ON THE I

"Starboard!"

To Kath

who gave the first opinion

ON THE EBB

Mike Peyton

fernhurst BOOKS

First published 1998 by

Fernhurst Books, Dukes Path, High Street,

Arundel, West Sussex, BN18 9AJ.

ISBN 1 898660 53 0

Design by Creative Byte
Printed by Hillman Printers, Frome

Printed and bound in Great Britain

Acknowledgements
**These cartoons are published with the kind permission of
Practical Boat Owner and *Yachting Monthly*,
where they first appeared.**

Contents

Offshore

"Do you think he knows you're racing him?"

*"Picking up the South Knock by dead reckoning gives
you a feeling of satisfaction you never get from G.P.S.."*

"That 'load of old balls' as you call it signifies 'towing and unable to deviate from my course'."

*"Funny, I only think about hiring
a liferaft when we're reefing."*

"And if you don't go easy we'll have
the 'run' but not the 'duty free'."

"Andy's having a quick look at the log –
he thinks there might be weed on the impeller."

"Never mind the article you read, what are you going to do?"

"We're pleased you came back, it makes us feel more seamanlike."

Home waters

"I'll bet the bonehead who wrote the piece on the joys of winter sailing isn't out."

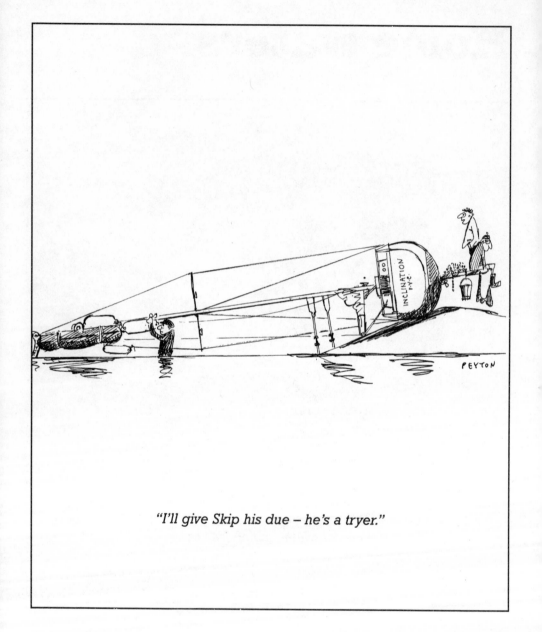

"I'll give Skip his due – he's a tryer."

"Not a lot of Christmas spirit in that lot, Joe."

"Starboard tack or not, I think you're pushing your luck."

"He's found the channel skip."

"They never mention this in their articles on winter sailing."

"Wake Skip and tell him the wind he said
would keep us offshore has shifted."

"Can you remember the name of the boat that was rafted alongside?"

"There's times I wish I'd never read Maurice Griffiths."

"What pleasure they see in golf beats me."

"What do you mean 'just got to run before it'?"

"It's the dockmaster on the VHF.
Do we know we've left the sidelights on?"

"Well at least it's stopped her dragging."

Gone foreign

"Hello Peter! You were sleeping so soundly after getting us here we hadn't the heart to wake you."

"I'm glad we met. It's been
a very pleasant evening."

"You know, I sometimes wish it would rain."

"I dropped the hook here to stretch my legs 15 years ago."

"I don't care whether it's a Sirocco, a Meltemi or a Mistral; it wasn't mentioned in the brochure."

"Oh, I forgot to mention we did hit......."

*"We're going to discuss the Cruise in
Company in the clubhouse."*

"It's Dover Coastguard. 'To any yacht converging on the Calais Approach buoy, there are eleven others.....'"

Back home

"Relax, I know the depth over the sill to a millimetre."

"We're going ashore again, old chap.
Can we bring you anything back?"

"I assure you sir, for marina cred........"

"I saw it first!"

"I wonder what this season will bring."

"I bet that's ruined someone's weekend."

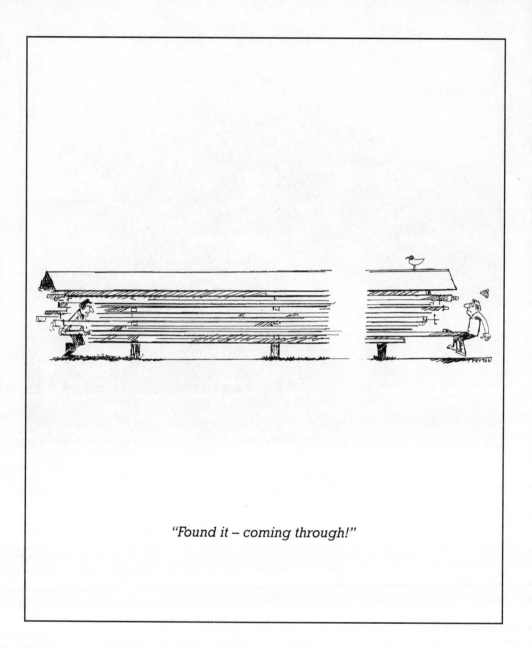

"Found it – coming through!"

*"They must have left their guide dog
at home when they bought it."*

"Pity you were stuck in the office over the weekend.
Force four, blazing sunshine......"

*"You haven't moved a dustbin liner
with two sleeping bags in it?
This one is full of gash."*

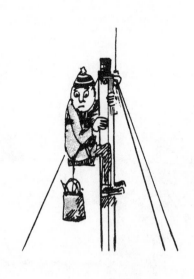

"Pity about the weather, Skip, when we're
all psyched up for a weekend's work."

"Radio check please."

"Well, thought of a name yet?"

"Mums's ever so keen for you to get afloat."

With the ladies

*"Perhaps they are characterless
Tupperware boxes but I bet they don't
have to sleep in their oilskins."*

*"If you want to know, your actual words were
'A touch of astern Darling'."*

*"What d'you mean it could get uncomfortable
when the tide turns?"*

"It's the office."

*"It's a pity your enthusiasm for catching
the tides can't be transferred to catching
the eight-thirty."*

*"Don't you know? Four Fastnets, a Yachtmaster Examiner
and City and Guilds in boat building.
She makes me sick."*

"But why take the dodgers off?"

"Initially I was dead set against having a conservatory."

"Yes, that's it, a taxi to the airport."

AS IT WAS.... A nostalgic glance back to the good/bad old days of yachting with some of Peyton's early cartoons, for which he has written a postscript.

It was the end of an era. In those pre-marina days, harbours were still considered as places of refuge for all seafarers and invariably free. One soon got to know the quiet corners where one could tie up and leave the boat for a few days though, as the cartoon shows, times were changing. A man-sized rubbing strake, which most boats had, and ample scooter tyres were recommended. I can never remember locking up the boat, mainly because she was often moved and whoever moved her might want to use the engine or get out more warps. From my moorings at Fambridge on the Crouch, I considered Torquay about the financial limit of my season's cruising, not because of harbour charges, but because of the train fare for two and two halves on a Friday night from London to get to the boat, and the same on Monday morning, plus breakfast on the train, to get back. It always seemed a very civilised way to start the week and the train timetable was as essential as the tide table. I thought then, and still do, that the biggest anchor most boats have is a car.

A cartoon of a more earthy era. Bucket and chuckit was the accepted norm in those pre-pushpit and pulpit days – though boom gallows were there to hang on to. One undisputed and sadly missed feature about a bucket was that it never, but never, got blocked up. One up from a bucket was a thunder box, almost always in the forepeak. The bucket fitted inside so it could be used in comfort without getting a circular impression on one's hindquarters. A friend told me he was once using his thunder box with his upper half protruding through the fore-hatch through necessity, because of the size of his boat. He was sitting there with his arms folded on the deck and at peace with the world as he faced his nearest and dearest, who was at the tiller. As his eyes wandered around the boat he noticed something in the cockpit and remarked to his wife, 'Strange, I didn't know we had two buckets on board.' His wife looked him in the eyes and replied, 'We haven't!'

Ply was the 'in' material and this class of boat was the base of the yachting pyramid. Crouching headroom was the phrase, gumboots the gear, the warm glow of the cabin lamp a fact of life, just as was the hissing and smell of the gimballed primus. It was the owners of these Silhouettes, Debutantes, Alacritys, etc who thronged the aisles of Earls Court and dreamed of winning the Pools. Ten thousand pounds would buy you a state-of-the-art blue water cruiser, with all the bells and whistles of the day. I must confess I once broke up such a domestic scene as is depicted here when, through a moment of inattention tacking through some moorings, the heavy old gaff cutter I owned at the time took charge. Her bobstay cut into the cabin like a chain-saw and it was almost a massacre.

It is difficult in these pressurised days to visualise having a Prime Minister who had time to race offshore and could be away from the Commons long enough to win the Sydney-Hobart Race. I believe in his spare time Sir Edward Heath even played the organ. I exchanged glares with him one Burnham Week when "Morning Cloud" took the wind of the Stella I was crewing as we approached a mark. I drew it straight and the caption, which was approximately what my skipper said, only had a couple of 'effings' missing which were considered unprintable.

Old workboats were a way for impecunious yachtsmen to get afloat and reverse sheer was the flavour of the month, providing freeboard outside and headroom inside. I bought an old working boat myself, but from Holland where there were hundreds for sale, owing to the polderising of the then Zuider Zee. I think I gave £400 for her. She was basically a 40ft open boat and still had a fish well. Though the engine gave up the ghost at Ijmuiden, she had plenty of sails. The trip was in November and was a mixture of fog and too much wind for comfort. My crew on that trip summed it up in one phrase. He had just finished his National Service as a midshipman in an aircraft carrier which had been showing the flag in the Caribbean with Governors' receptions, etc. As we parted, in reply to my query 'Enjoy the trip?' he said: 'Well, shall we say it wasn't like the aircraft carrier.'

This cartoon was a comment on the unofficial French refuse disposal system of the day. The official system of sewage disposal was more or less the same, but far more potent and systematic, invariably discharging into the harbour at High Water. One of my strongest memories of Calais Harbour in those distant days was of its stench and of one particular night spent jilling around the dangerous proximity to other British yachts. In dangerous proximity because we were all trying to keep in the same stretch of water, close to a Scandinavian timber ship that was tied alongside the quay. It was like a huge air freshener as it gave off an aroma redolent of resin and the tang of pine forests – an aromatic oasis in a night that reeked of the end product of thousands of French culinary efforts and on which the ebb had made, as yet, no impression.

"I generally give them an hour to get
comfortable before I wake them up
and tell them they can't lie there."

*"And in future remember,
you don't chuck the bucket."*

"And I said, 'Naturally, at £10,000
one would assume the engine and sails
would be optional extras'."

"He might win his class but if he doesn't
move over soon he's lost one vote."

"Hogged? She's not hogged,
she's got a reverse shear."

"Oops. Pardon Monsieur."

One of the earliest types of sailing hat was introduced into this country by Scandinavian cruising yachtsmen about the year 880. Originally, the hat had three horns, symbolising the three main interests of the sailing men of that time: rape, pillage and murder. This earlier model could also be used for beach barbecues, and some scholars assert that it was the forerunner, or at least influenced the design of, the Baby Blake, which ultimately usurped it. However, as murder fell out of fashion, two horns became the norm, and it was at this

stage of its development that it became the initial link, or half-way stage, in the transition from the tiller to wheel steering. Due to helmsmen who couldn't tell their larboard from their starboard through having used a tiller for so long, it also gave the English language the phrase 'on the horns of a dilemma'.

Some experts assume that the phrase
'a square peg in a round hole'
also derives from this period; all
Scandinavians having, as is well-
known, square heads, whereas tiller
posts were normally round. The hat
finally went out of favour when
synthetic materials were introduced
which were waterproof, didn't rust
and could breathe. The last vestige
of this traditional hat could be seen
at the beginning of this century in
the varnished bowlers that were, for
a time, in vogue with the small group
of fashion-conscious barge skippers
of the East Coast.

Night watches

"Well, at least the boat's insured."

"I know these waters pretty well."

*"The shore lights are going out?
None of your business, just keep winching."*

"It's OK, we're still in the channel
– there's a moored boat ahead."

"It will be somewhere over there –
and leave it to starboard because
it marks the edge of the sands."

"Just keep those leading lights in line."

"Do you ever think we're stupid?"

These things do happen

*"I'm doing Drama this year,
I got my Yachtmaster last year."*

*"Obviously I don't want to commit myself
until I get my RYA Day Skipper Theory."*

"We're a partner short in Latin-American class.
Any takers?

*"D'you know, last weekend Joyce actually showed
interest in getting a bigger boat."*

"Daddy's just going to nip down to the boat
and fit his Christmas present."

"I know where I am with it."

*"...... and then she said 'I hope your boat sinks'
and I snapped."*

*"Reading between the lines I'd say the tide didn't make enough,
he decided to take a chance, then lost his bottle."*

"*Empty it quick, I want it back!*"

"Admitted she's not the best under sail but she has the power to get you out of troub......"

"Well, at least the fog's lifted."

"*Quick, get a turn on him.*"

"You don't think it's Freudian?"